Incognito

Discovering God in Everyday Moments

Casey Jordan

Published by Mountaintop Publishing

Copyright © 2021 Casey Jordan

All rights reserved.

ISBN: 9798737664268

caseyjordan.com

To my Mama – who taught me to read.

To my Daddo – who taught me to write.

I love you forever.

Introduction

"We may ignore, but we can nowhere evade, the presence of God. The world is crowded with Him. He walks everywhere *incognito*. And the *incognito* is not always hard to penetrate. The real labor is to remember, to attend. In fact, to come awake. Still more, to remain awake."[1] — C.S. Lewis

This little book is about just that – coming awake.

It's a collection of stories and experiences.

It's about family and friends and strangers.

It's about travel and adventure.

It's about books I've read and shows I've watched.

But mostly it's about how God has taught and shaped me in the everyday moments.

Following Jesus is a day in and day out experience. Relationship with Him is both incomprehensibly extraordinary and astonishingly ordinary.

He's there through the highs and the lows. He's also there in the day-to-day.

I hope and pray that these stories – and what God has taught me through them – encourage you to pay attention to how God is teaching and shaping you every moment of every day.

The Great Egress

Long before P.T. Barnum joined with ringmaster Anthony Bailey to form "the Greatest Show on Earth," he had another, not entirely unrelated, career.

In 1841, Barnum opened a museum in downtown Manhattan that featured a wealth of peculiar attractions and intriguing exhibits.

The museum became so popular that Barnum began turning people away – an unfortunate decision that was obviously bad for business. He had to figure out a way to keep people from lingering too long so he could accommodate more visitors.

He came up with a brilliant plan.

Barnum printed large posters proclaiming, "This Way to the Great Egress!"

Arrows directed the curious customers towards a mysterious door near the back of the building. Anxious to see what was sure to be the most extraordinary of attractions, visitors made their way through the other exhibits a little more quickly.

When, finally, they came to the door marked "Egress," they excitedly stepped through, only to find themselves outside of the museum.

"Egress," it turns out, means "Exit."

Caught up in what comes next, I often miss what is right in front of me.

The promises of the future often distract me from the experience of the present. Concern about where I am going often keeps me from trusting God where I am in this very moment.

Let's keep moving forward, but let's not stop experiencing.

Let's keep planning, but not stop acting.

Let's keep preparing, but not stop living.

As Jim Elliot once wrote, "Wherever you are, be all there."

Die Walking

One of the most fascinating books I've ever read is "The Lost City of Z" by David Grann. It tells of British explorer Percy Fawcett's epic search in the early 1900s for the legendary city of Z, supposedly buried deep in the Amazon.

On one particularly treacherous venture into the jungle, Fawcett's exploration party ran out of food and, after days of trekking on empty stomachs, soon grew weak with hunger. More susceptible than ever to disease and infection, many developed severe fevers. Any hope of getting out alive, much less finding Z, began to deteriorate.

One of the men, unable to take another step under the weight of sickness and exhaustion, collapsed against a tree and begged Fawcett to leave him to die.

"No," said Fawcett. "If we die, we'll die walking."[2]

If we die, we'll die walking.

Most of us will never explore the Amazon (though if you happen to be planning a trip, please take me with you). Most of us won't ever face starvation or risk contracting malaria. The obstacles we face will be of a different sort.

But make no mistake. We *will* face obstacles.

We will face cancer and heart attacks and dementia.

We will experience layoffs and financial strains.

We will lose people we love.

When my earthly life expires and I stand before my God, I want to be able to say that I gave it everything I had.

I trusted Him through the trials.

I stayed faithful in the challenges.

I didn't collapse in the difficulties.

I want to die walking.

How about you?

Declaring Forgiveness

In an episode of The Office, a comedic television series on life at a mid-sized paper supply company, branch manager Michael Scott runs into some serious financial troubles. One of the accountants, Oscar, suggests that he declare bankruptcy.

Michael takes Oscar's advice literally. He marches out to face his employees and loudly says, "I DECLARE BANKRUPTCY!"

He returns to his office, satisfied that he has done what he needed to do.

A moment later, Oscar reappears in Michael's doorway. "Hey, I just wanted you to know that you can't just say the word 'bankruptcy' and expect anything to happen," he says, to which Michael responds, "I didn't *say* it, I *declared* it."[3]

I wonder if sometimes we think about forgiveness like Michael thought of bankruptcy. We declare our forgiveness, thinking that by simply saying the words something has changed.

Forgiveness is so much more than words we say.

Forgiveness means deciding to cancel a debt.

Forgiveness means that we let go of what we think we deserve.

Forgiveness means that we lay down the right to get even.

Forgiveness means that we stop resurrecting the hurt years after the fact.

It is not enough to declare forgiveness with our words.

We must also declare forgiveness with our lives.

Jesus declared forgiveness by giving up His.

How can we do less?

A Land Called Nothing

Just off Route 93, situated in the Arizona desert that separates Phoenix and Las Vegas, is a six-acre land called Nothing. Nothing is, appropriately, a ghost town.

Established in 1977, Nothing for years struggled to gain traction. Alas, with no running water, much less a sewer system, and no electricity, Nothing seemed to prophesy its own demise.

In the decades that have passed since the citizens of Nothing finally abandoned their fated town, many have come and tried to make something out of Nothing. But attempts to bring the dead town to life have inevitably failed.

A sign that once greeted visitors still stands.

It reads, "The staunch citizens of Nothing are full of hope, faith and believe in the work ethic. Thru the years, these dedicated people had faith in Nothing, hoped for Nothing, worked at Nothing, for Nothing."

You've got to admire the honesty.

If *you* were being honest, what would you say is the object of your faith, the essence of your hope, the reason for your work?

If the answer is anything other than Jesus, it is as good as Nothing.

You see, it was Jesus that spoke *everything* into being out of a vast *nothing*.

Imagine what He could do with *your* life. Imagine what He could do with mine.

Let's stop putting our faith in Nothing. Let's stop banking our hopes on Nothing. Let's stop working for Nothing.

He wants to raise our ghost town lives. He wants to bring the dead back to life.

But we have to leave behind the Nothing we've been clinging to. He has so much more in store for us.

Legacy

My great-grandmother – Grandma Gertie, as we called her – was one of the godliest women I've ever known.

She had just turned ninety when her health began to fail.

My family and I made the six-hour drive from St. Louis, Missouri to her retirement home in North Manchester, Indiana to say our goodbyes. She was as alert and sharp as ever and we spent the week laughing and talking, playing games and listening to her stories. She had so many stories.

When it was time to go home, I was allowed to stay behind with my great-aunt Judi. We were together when a nurse called in the early hours to tell us that Grandma Gertie wasn't going to make it through the night.

I grabbed her Bible off her nightstand, and we hurried to the intensive care wing where she had spent her last few days. I wish I could remember what I read to her that night. I know it was from Psalms – she loved that book most.

I was holding her hand when she passed.

Gertie knew Jesus. She didn't just know *about* Him. She *knew* Him and she *loved* Him. I watched her take her last breath and realized that there was nothing that she wanted more than to be with Him and soon she would be.

I also realized, in that moment, that if I died I wouldn't be with Him. I wasn't a Christian. I knew *about* Jesus, but I didn't *know* Jesus and I didn't love Him.

I wish I could tell you I made the decision to accept the grace of God that night. I wish I could tell you that right then I put my trust in Him. I wish I could tell you from that day forward He was the object of my faith and the reason for my hope. I wish I could tell you all that, but I can't.

I took her Bible home with me. I began reading the notes she had made in the margins of nearly every page. Then, I started reading the words she had been reflecting on.

I read about the love of God and the grace Jesus offered. I read about forgiveness and hope and joy and peace. Grandma Gertie had all of those things. I wanted them, too. So, after months of God relentlessly drawing me towards Himself – through His Word and through Gertie's example – I finally accepted Christ.

Witnessing her faith encouraged mine. Watching her life changed mine.

There are people witnessing our faith and watching our lives.

What is it they see?

We all leave a legacy.

The question is what kind of legacy we will leave.

The Curse of Zeigarnik

There is this concept in psychological research known as the Zeigarnik Effect. The basic idea is that people have a drive to complete tasks rather than leave them unfinished.

It's why loyalty cards are so effective.

It's why we loathe having an inbox full of unread emails.

It's why we feel a sense of accomplishment when we check something off our to-do lists. (And, confession, if I complete a task that *wasn't* on my list, I'll add it just so I can cross it off.)

It's why we don't like to be interrupted when we're in the middle of something.

The Zeigarnik Effect is key to being a functional and productive person.

Can you imagine how little we would accomplish without this drive to finish things? We would probably never take out the garbage, remember to go grocery shopping, or bother with any of the less exciting tasks necessary to living as a properly socialized adult.

But there's a dark side to the Zeigarnik Effect.

You see, the Zeigarnik Effect impacts what we do, but can also blind us who we are – and who we are becoming.

We can easily become more focused on productivity than people, more concerned with results than relationships, and more taken by completion than character.

To put what we *do* ahead of who we *are* is to put the cart before the horse.

What we do ought to flow out of who we are, not the other way around.

Maybe we need fewer to-do lists.

Maybe we need a to-*be* list.

Maybe we need to spend less time on tasks – important though they may be – and spend more time on cultivating generosity, walking in faithfulness, exercising patience, and making peace with others.

Don't fall victim to the curse of Zeigarnik.

Resist the urge to measure your life by your productivity.

Resolve to spend time on who you are and who you are becoming.

When Love is at Stake

It's crazy what people will do when love is at stake.

In 2007, former astronaut Lisa Nowak got caught up in a dramatic love triangle. She was in love with a man who was in love with another woman. So, overcome with anger, she donned an adult diaper and set out on a cross-country road trip to confront her rival. The media, of course, had a field day with the story. It didn't help that she was armed with a BB gun and a black wig.

Commenting on this woman's absurd behavior, cartoonist Tim Kreider quipped, "When love is at stake, you do not waste time on rest stops."[4]

Nowak, it seems, was not so much driven by love as by jealousy.

There's really no defending her behavior, given that there is reason to believe she intended to attack her ex-boyfriend's new love interest.

But as I thought about the foolish love of this woman, I thought about a greater love that, to so many, looks equally foolish.

"The message of the cross," wrote the apostle Paul, "is foolish to those who are headed for destruction."[5]

And I can see why.

On the cross, a man who claimed to be God hung naked and bloody.

The media, of course, had a field day with the story.

They humiliated and ridiculed him, laughed at him and mocked him, as he slowly suffocated.

Why in the world would anyone willingly submit themselves to something as scandalous as the cross?

Love.

Love compelled the God of the universe to step down from His throne and don human skin.

Love compelled Him to befriend the lowest of the low, to engage the outcasts, to dine with prostitutes and tax collectors.

Love is what compelled Him to sacrifice His life for the very ones who murdered Him.

It's *crazy* what people will do when love is at stake.

Learning a Few Moves

If you've never listened to the stand-up comedy of Brian Regan, you need to.

He once did a hilarious bit on dancing.

"I've learned a few moves, you know, to fit in. You know what I haven't figured out? How to have fun."[6]

That pretty much sums up my relationship with dancing.

Learning a few moves is how I survive wedding receptions which, with high school dances mercifully behind me, are the only time I dance. I've gotten pretty good at rocking side to side and, every once in a while, I'm even on beat.

But I've never learned how to have fun doing it.

There's nothing wrong with learning a few moves to make those inevitable social situations a little more bearable.

There are times, though, when there's more on the line.

There are times when the stakes are much, much higher.

Sometimes, learning a few moves means forfeiting our integrity.

Sometimes, fitting in means compromising the truth.

Sometimes, earning the approval of others means sacrificing our values.

It's not worth it.

Surrendering who we are and what we believe to keep, momentarily, from standing out is not worth it.

The cost is exponentially greater than the reward.

I will probably never enjoy dancing. I'll probably never fit in on the dance floor.

But that's okay.

It's only my pride at stake – not my character.

Spiritual Hoarding

In recent years, the world of hoarding has captured the attention of millions, as evidenced by more than a couple of shows dedicated to the phenomenon.

The camera pans over piles of half-eaten pizzas, empty shampoo bottles, broken electronics, and newspaper coupons from 1967.

The home of a hoarder is anything but inviting. There is no room for company. It is not conducive to relationship. The home of a hoarder is, to put it bluntly, disgusting.

In the course of a one-hour episode, the chaotic life of a hoarder is transformed. As the mountains of trash are disassembled, a new space emerges. Space for friendship. Space for productive work and peaceful rest. Space for life to begin again.

While hoarding might make for interesting, though somewhat debasing, television, there is nothing compelling about *spiritual* hoarding.

It's hoarding of a different sort.

It's what happens when we accumulate information but fail to experience transformation.

When we collect knowledge but fail to apply it to our lives.

When we amass heads full of facts and data but fail to cultivate hearts full of love and grace.

It's what makes for great Bible trivia contestants, but lousy Christians.

If left unchecked, the life of a spiritual hoarder will eventually become cluttered with pride, piled with judgmentalism, and coated with a thick layer of self-righteousness.

The heart of a spiritual hoarder is anything but inviting. There is no room for company. It is not conducive to relationship. The heart of a spiritual hoarder is, to put it bluntly, disgusting.

Hoarders of any sort are usually unaware of the problem and wouldn't know where to begin if they were. Hoarders need an intervention.

Consider this an intervention – of your heart and mine.

Help is available through the grace of God and the support and encouragement of godly friends, if only we would ask for and accept it.

It will take more than an hour to disassemble the build-up of spiritual hoarding. It will take more blood, sweat, and tears than we anticipate to break through the accumulation of narcissism caked on our hearts. But, over time, a new space will emerge.

Space for friendship. Space for productive work and peaceful rest. Space for life - the life God intended for us - to begin again.

Six Words

William Borden was the heir to an enormous family fortune. When he graduated from high school in 1904, his parents sent him on a trip through Europe, the Middle East, and Asia.

The experience profoundly changed Borden. The pain and suffering he saw compelled him to become a missionary.

His family and friends couldn't believe that he would throw away his opportunity at wealth to become a missionary. But he was determined.

In the back of his Bible, he wrote two words.

"No reserves."

Borden returned to the States and began taking courses at Yale.

It was evident to everyone that there was something different about him. His faith surpassed that of his classmates. He once invited a friend to meet him each morning for prayer and Bible study.

In four years, what began as two friends getting together had expanded into over a thousand students meeting daily in study groups.

After graduating from college, Borden was offered a number of high-paying jobs. He turned them all down. He went instead to Princeton Seminary to prepare for the mission field.

He wrote two more words in his Bible.

"No retreats."

When he finished his studies at Princeton, he set off to China.

He hoped to work with Muslims and so he stopped first in Egypt to study Arabic.

There he contracted spinal meningitis and, a month later, William Borden was dead at the age of 25.

The news was cabled back to the United States and, as Borden's biographer, Mary Taylor, wrote, "A wave of sorrow went round the world… Borden not only gave [away] his wealth, but himself, in a way so joyous and natural that it [seemed] a privilege rather than a sacrifice."[7]

His Bible was recovered. He had written two more words beneath "No reserves" and "No retreats."

"No regrets."

Six words. Three resolutions. One purpose.

What would happen if we all lived with such a determined and clear purpose?

It would change the world.

Freedom and Fishbowls

In his 1913 dictionary, Noah Webster defined freedom, in part, as the "exemption from the power and control of another."[8]

Freedom, we have come to believe, means that we are not bound to anyone or anything.

In our highly individualistic culture, we place great value on such independence.

But what if we're wrong?

What if we have misjudged our reality and misunderstood true freedom?

Consider a fish in a fishbowl.

It would be ridiculous for a mother fish to say to her baby fish, "You can be anything you want to be." That is simply untrue. The fish lives in a finite reality, with finite opportunities.

True freedom, our culture might say, would be to shatter the confining bowl and to explore the world beyond.

What, though, would happen if the fish *did* manage to break out of his glass world?

He would be unable to survive his newfound "freedom."

He would suffocate.

The walls of his fishbowl, it would turn out, were not *hindering* his freedom but *maximizing* it.

We too live in a finite world.

Praise God, He has given us a world far richer than a fishbowl.

But it is finite all the same.

There are boundaries to our reality. These boundaries, drawn by a God infinite both in love and knowledge, are for our good and His glory.

True life, true freedom, is found *within* His boundaries.

To believe there is life outside them is to be deceived.

Can we break through the boundaries? Sure we can.

But, when we do, like a fish trying to escape his fishbowl, we find that it leads only to death and despair.

Wonder

As I was waiting for my flight from St. Louis to Charlotte to take off, I noticed a little girl sitting across the aisle from me. She was looking out the window with all the intensity a three-year-old could muster as her mom pointed out the other planes taking off.

"Where do you think they're going?" she would ask.

"I don't know, mama!" the little girl would say. "But it looks like so much fun!"

When our plane started moving, I watched her eyes grow wide as she took her mom's hand.

"It's our turn! It's our turn! Here we go!"

We started down the runway and I could hear her giggling as we picked up speed. As the wheels lifted off the concrete, she let out the most joyful squeal I've ever heard in my life. It was the sound of pure delight, pure excitement at what seemed to her the most amazing adventure. She was totally unaware that people were watching her. She was lost in her wonder.

I don't know when I lost that sense of wonder.

I've traveled a lot in my three decades. It's really no big deal anymore. Actually, it's become something of a hassle - canceled flights, maintenance delays, bad airplane food.

I always look forward to the destination, but the journey is really just a necessary annoyance.

I can treat life that way, too. As an inconvenience. As a means to an end. Always looking forward to the next big thing, but often forgetting that most of life happens in between the big things.

G.K. Chesterton once wrote, "Because children have abounding vitality, because they are in spirit fierce and free, therefore they want things repeated and unchanged. They always say, 'Do it again'; and the grown-up person does it again until he is nearly dead. For grown-up people are not strong enough to exult in monotony. But perhaps God is strong enough to exult in monotony. It is possible that God says every morning, 'Do it again' to the sun; and every evening, 'Do it again' to the moon. It may not be automatic necessity that makes all daisies alike; it may be that God makes every daisy separately but has never got tired of making them. It may be that He has the eternal appetite of infancy; for we have sinned and grown old, and our Father is younger than we."⁹

Children understand a part of God that we grown-ups have long forgotten.

They understand *wonder*.

As you go about your day and as I go about mine, let's remember what it was like to exult in monotony. Let's look for opportunities to delight in the journey. Let's recapture the sense of wonder that growing old left behind.

Fairy Tales

Why is it that children love fairy tales?

Perhaps because children know something we adults do not. Perhaps we adults "know" that fairy tales are make believe, while children know we live inside of one.

The biblical story is the most captivating fairy tale ever written – only it's true.

There is a great King, ruling and reigning with His Son, the good Prince. The Prince longs to be married, but His would-be bride is held captive by a mighty Dragon.

You see, the bride was once a loyal subject of the great King, but long ago rebelled. She enslaved herself to the Dragon, submitted only to his will.

The Prince's love compelled Him to rescue His captive bride, so He set out after her. He defeated the Dragon at the cost of His own life. And His bride, finally free from her bondage, mourned His death.

But the story was far from over.

The King gets the last word.

When all hope seemed to be lost, the great King, in a dramatic plot twist, raised the good Prince from the dead.

The Prince reclaimed His throne and married the bride for whom He willingly gave His life. And, loved and cherished by the great King, they lived happily ever after.

Enthralling, is it not?

But this is no mere fairy tale.

This is my story and yours.

For those on the side of the King and His Son, there is a "happily ever after."

For those on the side of the Dragon, there awaits death and destruction.

We live somewhere between the resurrection of the good Prince and the final reclaiming of His throne.

In the meantime, we must declare our allegiance, either to the defeated Dragon or to the victorious Prince.

Choose wisely, my friends.

Lawnmowers

The moment I start my lawnmower, a little face appears in the window next door. Within seconds, Karl is by my side, smiling up at me through his pacifier.

Karl is three years old and for the last few months, he has "helped" me tend to my lawn every Saturday morning.

As I mow strip after strip, Karl follows behind with his own plastic lawnmower. It doesn't trim a single blade of grass, but it does shoot out bubbles as he totters along. Every once in a while, he'll go rogue and start mowing in circles, but as I stay on track, cutting in straight, neat lines, Karl usually falls back in step behind me.

He doesn't say much, but his innocent giggle tells me he is enjoying every moment of our mostly wordless time together as much as I am.

Every time we work side by side, bringing a sort of beauty out of the chaos of an overgrown yard, I can't help but wonder if the joy I experience watching Karl imitate me is anything like the joy God experiences when I imitate Him.

After all, it's what I was made to do.

The Bible says that I was created in the image of God.

So were you.

We were not created to *be* God, of course, but to serve as His representatives to a watching world.

To be merciful as He is merciful.

To uphold justice as He upholds justice.

To give as He gives.

To serve as He serves.

To love as He loves.

We are at our best when we are imitating the heart and character of God and He delights in seeing us at our best (though He still loves us at our worst).

Let's imitate Him. It brings delight to His heart and – honestly – there is no more joyful way to live.

Loneliness Imagined

In 1978, Jim Davis debuted one of the most beloved cartoons of all time – *Garfield*.

Garfield is the original "Grumpy Cat." When he's not eating lasagne, he is sleeping, complaining, or pulling practical jokes on Odie, a fun-loving, but gullible, dog. Both Garfield and Odie belong to Jon Arbuckle, an awkward bachelor, who spends more time talking to his pets than he does talking to other humans.

For the most part, the three live together in a mundane, relatively peaceful, existence.

However, in October of 1989, Davis decided to press pause on the light-hearted themes of *Garfield* to write a Halloween series that dealt with fear.

Davis conducted an informal survey to find out what people are afraid of.

The most common response was loneliness.

So, Davis crafted a comic in which Garfield wakes up to find that both Jon and Odie have deserted him.

He is cold, hungry, and utterly alone. He can't believe they are gone. He begins to panic and finally, in his desperation, cries out, "I don't want to be alone!"

The next frame cuts to Jon and Odie, breaking Garfield out of his daze by offering him breakfast. It was all in his mind. Garfield, overcome with relief, throws himself on Jon and says, "Who needs it? I need *you*!"

The final frame is haunting. Davis writes, "An imagination is a powerful tool. It can tint memories of the past, shape perceptions of the present, or paint a future so vivid that it can entice... or terrify, all depending upon how we conduct ourselves today..."[10]

Davis was onto something.

I wonder how often we feel – or imagine – we are alone, when, all along, there are people ready and waiting to know and love us. If only we would open our eyes and break from our daze.

I wonder how often we, who have been brought back into a relationship with God by the life, death, and resurrection of Jesus, forget that we are *never* alone. He has promised to be with us *always* – and God keeps His promises.

If you feel alone, know that you are not or, at least, you don't have to be. There is a God ready and waiting to know and love you, if only you would open your eyes and break from your daze.

And remember, an imagination is a powerful tool.

End of Construction

Ruth Bell was born in 1920 to medical missionary parents serving in China. She came to know Jesus at a young age and always thought she would remain single.

She planned, like her parents, to serve as a missionary in Asia.

God, though, had other plans.

In 1940, while enrolled at Wheaton College, she met a man named Billy. In 1943, the two were married and Ruth Bell became Ruth Bell Graham.

Neither could have predicted the adventure ahead. Neither could have known how God would use them to advance the cause of Christ.

Through their ministry, hundreds of millions of people heard the message of Jesus.

Ruth passed away in 2007 and was buried at the Billy Graham Library in Charlotte, North Carolina.

Next to her tombstone is a plaque that says, "While riding down the highway years ago, Ruth noticed a sign beside the road: 'END OF CONSTRUCTION – THANK YOU FOR YOUR PATIENCE.' With a smile, she said that these were the words she wanted on her gravestone."

And they are.

I've been under construction for handful of decades now. By the grace of God, there has been a lot of progress, but there is also still a lot of work left to be done.

I'm more generous than I used to be, but I still hold tightly to what I perceive to be mine.

I'm more forgiving than I used to be, but I can still hold a grudge.

I'm more faithful to Jesus than I used to be, but I still wander.

I'm more selfless than I used to be, but I still put myself first most of the time.

I'm not alone in that. None of us has arrived. None of us is all that God created us and saved us to be. None of us is without fault and failure. None of us is without sin.

We're all still under construction.

Let's be patient with one another.

Off with His Head

In the 2010 remake of Alice in Wonderland, there's a scene in which the evil Red Queen discovers that her tarts have been stolen.

To say that the Queen has a bit of a temper would be an understatement.

She also, apparently, really loves tarts. When she realizes that they are gone, she sort of loses her marbles.

Infuriated, she bursts into the hallway and begins inspecting each of her servants, intent on finding the perpetrator. When, finally, the guilty servant is found, exposed by a hint of raspberry jam at the corner of his mouth, she bellows, "Off with his head!"

Every time I watch that scene, I just want to pull the Queen aside and say, "Look, I know he stole your tarts and all, but I *think* you might be overreacting just a little."

It's comical, of course, but the truth is that I often overreact.

And when I do, it is anything but comical.

The man that just cut me off in traffic without using his turn signal? Off with his head!

The woman that won't stop talking excessively loudly on her phone in an otherwise quiet waiting room? Off with her head!

The guy at the gym that sits on the machines in between sets so that no one else can use them? Off with his head!

I could go on.

You probably could too.

Thanks to a good bit of socializing, my irritation and impatience rarely surface. Yet there they are - right on the edge of my heart.

And therein lies the problem- my *sinful* heart.

The content of my heart comes pouring out when I get bumped.

It spills over and exposes who I really am. It is evident in the words that escape my lips and even in the words left unspoken.

If I am the problem, though, I cannot also be the solution. A sinful heart cannot remedy a sinful heart.

Jesus conquered my sin on the cross – and He conquered yours.

I don't look as much like Jesus as I want to – but I look more like Him now than I did a year ago. He keeps on changing me.

How is He changing you?

Shine Like Stars

I spent a fall living in Colorado – learning, studying, working, connecting.

I still think about that season of my life almost every day – the lessons, the memories, the people. Those months changed me. There are so many stories I could share, but there's one particular memory that has stayed with me.

One weekend, my friends and I went camping in the Rockies.

We drove for what seemed like hours before finally arriving at our campsite.

We unloaded our gear and laughed as we fumbled with our tents, trying to assemble them in the dark.

We sang songs and told stories and talked about what God had done over our last few months together.

After eating our campfire-cooked meal, we pulled out our sleeping bags and situated ourselves on the cold, hard ground. As my head eased onto my pillow, I looked up at the night sky.

What I saw took my breath away.

Out of the dark sky burst a million stars. Without the ambient light of the city, they seemed to shine magnificently bright.

"Do everything," wrote Paul to the Philippians, "without grumbling or arguing, so that you may become blameless and pure, 'children of God without fault in a warped and crooked generation.' Then you will shine among them like stars in the sky, as you hold firmly to the word of life."[11]

All of my life I've wanted to fit in, to be a part of the crowd. To be, well, normal.

Looking at the stars as I lay on the side of that mountain I understood, maybe for the first time, that I'm not supposed to fit in.

I'm *supposed* to be different – not for the sake of being different, but for the cause of Christ.

I'm supposed to live my life in such a way that, against the dark backdrop of a warped and crooked world, I shine with the radiant light of Jesus.

If you're a Christian, this is your calling, too. We, as a community, are to burst through the darkness as a million stars.

We are to be different.

Standing Together

I love historical fiction. I especially love anything written by Conn Iggulden.

A couple of years ago, a friend introduced me to his series on Genghis Khan. It was spectacular. So, I recently picked up his series on Julius Caesar. It, too, was spectacular. (I'm just starting his series on the War of Roses and it's every bit as good). But back to Julius Caesar.

During one escapade to wreak vengeance on a pirate sea craft early in his career, Julius lay awake, worrying that his legion would not prove up to the task. They were a relatively ragtag band of soldiers, with only a handful of professionally trained men. The rest were nothing more than enthusiastic peasants picked up at local port towns.

As Julius considered the battle to come, he comforted himself with the knowledge that his men would stand firm.

They had, after all, developed a strong comradery throughout their adventures.

"A man standing next to his friends cannot run for shame,"[12] thought Julius.

While I certainly don't condone wreaking vengeance on pirate sea crafts, I think Julius (well, Iggulden) had a point.

Standing next to friends elicits a confidence and courage unmatched by individual resolution. Perhaps that is, at least in part, why the Bible places such an emphasis on community.

God has given me the most remarkable friends over the years.

They have stood next to me through difficult seasons, major decisions, and change – lots of change.

They have challenged me to stand firm in my faith when it would be easier to desert.

They have loved me at my worst and see all that I could be – all that God intends for me to be.

They don't let me run for shame.

I pray you have friends like that. If you don't, I pray you find them.

And I pray you *are* that friend – for someone.

Represent

The departure time was approaching, and we still hadn't been assigned a gate, so I lingered around the departure board in my usual terminal at the Charlotte airport, waiting for my flight to St. Louis to update.

My family didn't know I was coming in for the weekend and I couldn't wait to see the look on their faces when I walked in the door (surprising them is the one this I miss about living in another city).

Instead of assigning us a gate, they delayed our flight by fifteen minutes. Then another fifteen. Then thirty. Three hours later, we boarded.

And, for thirty more minutes, we sat. No one came on the speaker to update us on the further delay. We didn't see a pilot or anything resembling a crew. Finally, a flight attendant emerged and informed us that they were fixing a minor maintenance issue and we would be off in no time.

Another twenty minutes passed.

People were clearly getting agitated.

If I'm being honest, I was too.

I was supposed to be home hours ago.

The man sitting next to me started to complain loudly about the poor communication (it really was pretty bad). The woman on the other side of me seemed to be struggling with the concept of personal space. The kid behind me started to kick my seat out of boredom.

Everything in me wanted to commiserate with the man on my right, elbow the woman on my left, and whack the kid behind me.

The only thing that kept me from being a complete jerk was my t-shirt.

I was wearing a shirt that bore the name of my church.

When I put on that shirt, I became a representative of my church. How I behaved, how I spoke, how I reacted would communicate something about my church and the kind of people that have aligned themselves with its mission.

It's like an athlete putting on his jersey.

It said, "This is who I play for. This is my team. This is who I represent."

As I sat on that hot, noisy plane, thinking about all of this, I realized that this is actually my every day.

When I wake up in the morning, the Bible says that I am to "put on Christ."

I play for Him. I am on His team. I represent Him. How I behave, how I speak, how I react communicates something about the kind of person that follows Him.

The question, of course, is whether or not I'm communicating what Jesus would have me communicate.

My motive for keeping calm in a frustrating airplane situation should not have been my t-shirt. It should have been Jesus.

I have aligned myself with His mission. And so now, I represent Him.

In everything.

Good Over Fast

A friend and I met at a local coffee shop to catch up. It was all small talk at first, but our conversation soon turned to traveling.

She began telling me about the time she and her husband spent in Europe.

She said they quickly noticed the Europeans seemed, on the whole, to be more fit than most Americans.

Local businesses would close down in the middle of the day so their employees could enjoy a long meal and it wasn't uncommon for dinner to stretch late into the night.

My friends couldn't understand how these people, who seemed to spend so much of their time eating, managed to stay so lean.

Finally, her husband decided to ask a waitress to explain it to him.

Her response was profound.

"You eat food fast," she said. "We eat good food."

She's right, I think.

We often opt for fast over good. We choose convenience over quality. We think more about efficiency than we do enjoyment.

And we are paying a price for those choices. Our health is suffering. Cancer and heart disease are prevalent. More than half of all Americans are on medication – many on more than one.

Certainly, food is not the only factor.

That's not really the point, though.

The point is our tendency for fast over good – a mentality that spills into other parts of our lives.

Particularly, our relationships.

Too often that's how we approach our friendships, our marriages, our children, and even God.

Relationships take work. They take investment. They take time. They are meant to be savored, cherished, enjoyed. When we prioritize convenience over community, we miss out on the goodness of relationships.

And we pay a price for that choice.

I'm going to choose to prioritize the good - the *better*. I hope you do too.

Slow down.

Savor the people in your life.

Take time to enjoy your relationships - including (and especially) with God.

Hot Pockets

Of all my (many) quirks, I probably get teased (mostly by my big brother) for my love of stand-up comedy the most.

That *might* be because I think that since I listen to a lot of comedy I, too, must be hilarious.

Apparently, it does not work that way.

But I digress.

The reason I love stand-up comedy is that it exposes ridiculous human behaviors through the lens of the mundane. We are bizarre creatures and don't even know it.

I went to see one of my favorite comedians – Jim Gaffigan – with a couple of friends. He is known for his bits on food and is perhaps best known for his bit on Hot Pockets.

If you've never had a Hot Pocket, congratulations. You are in an elite club that comprises seven other Americans.

Hot Pockets, as described by Gaffigan, are a Pop-Tart crust filled with nasty meat. There is also a vegetarian version for "people who don't want to eat meat, but still want diarrhea."

I don't think anyone is under any illusion that Hot Pockets are healthy. No one thinks they are doing their body any good by consuming a Hot Pocket. Yet, millions are sold every year.

"I've never eaten a Hot Pocket and afterwards thought 'I'm glad I ate that,'"[13] Gaffigan observes.

I listened (and laughed) as he talked about Hot Pockets, and thought about how I have made a lot of choices I *know* aren't good for me, exposing me as the ridiculous person I am.

I know I'm not doing my body – or soul – any good, but I keep making those terrible choices.

I've chosen to cling to jealousy and watched my gratitude erode.

I've chosen to be dishonest and watched trust deteriorate.

I've chosen selfishness and watched relationships break down.

I've never given into greed, arrogance, impatience, anger, disloyalty, or cowardice, and afterwards thought, "I'm glad I did that."

There's nothing funny about self-destruction.

I'm going to be more careful about what I let into my heart.

There is too much at stake.

Quicksand

Most of my childhood was spent playing with my two brothers in the beautiful woods behind our house.

We created elaborate imaginary worlds out there (think *Bridge to Terabithia*, only with a less tragic ending). We had our own system of currency (usually rocks – sandstones were like gold to us), our own medical practices (dirt and leaves, mostly), even our own sports ("mud-boarding," which involved gliding down the hills in our sneakers and only worked right after it rained).

Our many hours in the woods also gave us this sense of survival – we had to take care of ourselves in the dangerous backcountry of our suburban home. (In reality, our parents could see us through the living room window.)

Obviously, if we were going to survive in the deep wilderness, we needed survival books. Our favorite was *The Worst-Case Scenario Survival Handbook*.

You never knew when you'd need to escape the death-grip of quicksand.

The first step, by the way, is to not panic which means eight-year-old Casey probably wouldn't have made it to the second step.

I always thought quicksand would turn out to be a bigger problem than it has been thus far.

I've actually never even *seen* quicksand, much less been stuck in it. Yet, the fear was there. I would often imagine what a horrible death that would be. I would imagine the feeling of utter loneliness as I sunk into the darkness. Morbid, I know.

I'm not afraid of quicksand anymore. I've outgrown that.

I have adult fears now — about relationships, about finances, about health.

I spin my own worst-case scenarios. I catastrophize. I let my imagination run wild. Nothing feeds my fear like my imagination.

Throughout my life, most of what I feared would happen never did.

Life hasn't been perfect, by any means, but it also hasn't been as tragic as I thought it would be.

Yes, there is real tragedy and real pain and real worst-case scenarios.

But let's deal with those as they come and resolve to no longer waste ourselves on destructive fantasies.

The Object of Gratitude

Gratitude has been getting a lot of press lately.

Psychologists present research demonstrating the many mental and emotional benefits of practicing gratitude. Motivational speakers and productivity gurus talk about the value of incorporating gratitude into their daily routines. Publishing companies release gratitude journals sprinkled with inspirational quotes.

But there's something missing.

The *object* of gratitude.

Gratitude implies that a gift has been received. If a gift was received, then there must have been a *giver*.

Do you see what's been done?

We've made gratitude about the *receiver* rather than about the *giver*.

The *expression* of gratitude, as a response to the giver, has been turned into the *emotion* of gratitude, to further profit the receiver.

That's not gratitude.

It's selfishness.

The Bible tells us that God is the Giver of every good and perfect gift. He is the object of our gratitude. He is the recipient of our thanks.

I'm not opposed to practicing gratitude.

But don't buy into the hype that says you should practice gratitude because it's good for your mental and emotional health to engage in daily gratitude journaling.

Nonsense.

It's not about you.

You – and I – are recipients. We aren't grateful because it benefits us. We're grateful because we have been blessed by the Giver.

So, be grateful to the Giver – the God of the universe – for every good and perfect gift.

Orient your paise – orient your *gratitude* – towards Him.

The Joy of Gratitude

I sat down intending to write a profound reflection on gratitude one Thanksgiving morning.

I intended to compose beautiful words about what it means to give thanks.

I tried to focus on finding an eloquent way to describe what it means to be grateful.

But Annie just wanted me to play with her.

My six-month-old niece was scooting around at my feet. She let out a delighted squeal as she gripped my pant leg and tried to pull herself up. She looked at me with her big blue eyes and gave me a heart-melting, dimpled smile.

I put away my writing and got down on the floor.

Thanksgiving is about, well, giving thanks for all that God has done for us.

Gratitude, though, is more than what we say – it's how we live.

Gratitude is about thanking God for Annie and then getting down on the floor and enjoying the blessing of her little life.

Gratitude is about thanking God for your family and then savoring the laughter shared around the dinner table.

Gratitude is about thanking God for your friends and then treasuring the conversations over a cup of coffee.

It is expression *and* enjoyment.

Words of gratitude without a life of gratitude are empty.

Let's *express* our gratitude today and every day.

But let's not forget to *enjoy* what God has given.

The Middle of Stories

When Steve Jobs passed away in 2011, his sister, Mona Simpson, gave his eulogy.

I remember reading it in the New York Times the next day and something she said leapt off the page at me.

"We all — in the end — die in *medias res*. In the middle of a story. Of many stories."[14]

She's right.

But life, as well as death, happens in the middle of many stories.

People have moved in and out of mine.

Some stepped out of my story far too soon and others have overstayed their welcome.

Some have been a source of great joy and others have left pain and hurt in their wake.

Some have changed me in ways I can hardly explain and others I can barely remember.

But all have left their mark.

We live and die, work and play, laugh and grow, in the middle of stories, of many stories.

We shape each other's plots.

We impact each other's lives.

We change each other's stories.

What an incredible responsibility it is to know that, for better or worse, we leave a mark.

What mark will *you* leave?

What We Have Left

The hall burst in applause as Itzhak Perlman appeared on the stage, took up his violin, and nodded to the conductor.

A couple of bars into the first song, one of Perlman's strings snapped.

It would have been quite understandable for the great violinist to bring the concert to a brief halt so that he could change the string and continue as he had rehearsed.

But that's not what he did.

He paused only a moment before signaling to the conductor to start from where they left off.

Perlman resolved to perform his solo with only three strings.

He adjusted the notes in his head to accommodate the deficient instrument. When he was unable to find a comparable note on another string, he improvised.

The piece held together spectacularly.

When the final note rang out, the audience sat in silence for just a moment, astonished at what they had just witnessed.

Then, once again, they erupted into wild ovation.

Perlman waited until the noise died away before addressing the eager crowd.

"You know," he said, "sometimes it is the artist's task to find out how much beautiful music you can still make with what you have left."

Perlman had full awareness of his weaknesses and full mastery of his strengths.

He did not ignore the former, nor did he dismiss the latter.

We all have broken strings. We all have others still intact.

Artistic wisdom requires that we be both aware of our weaknesses and then learn to play to our strengths.

Only then can we make beautiful music with what we have left.

Buggy

If you've never read *Dilbert* before, you're missing out. It's really funny.

The comic pokes fun at corporate culture – culture that stifles productivity, fosters laziness, and awards incompetence.

Cartoonist Scott Adams – through this imaginary corporate world – makes remarkably astute observations about human behavior.

In one strip, Dilbert is meeting with his Pointy-Haired Boss and the company CEO to update them on a recurring set of internal business issues.

"I found the root cause of our problems," says Dilbert.

"It's people. They're buggy."[15]

They sure are.

I sure am.

We are the root cause of nearly all of our problems.

We are the root cause of our greatest miscommunications.

We are the root cause of a lot of unresolved conflict.

We are the root cause of most of our relational breakdowns.

We are all buggy.

It doesn't do us any good to pretend otherwise.

So, let's be gracious with one another.

Let's not be so hard on the flaws of other people.

Let's, instead, spend a little more time working on ours.

The Red Strokes

I hated the red pen.

You know the one I'm talking about.

The red pen that marked all my wrong answers. The one that boldly proclaimed every grammatical error. The mark that smugly declared the value of my efforts at the top of the page.

The red pen judged me.

A 2010 study led by a Tufts University graduate student named Michael Slepian tested the difference between using a red pen and a black pen.

"Participants in the study were given incomplete words and had to fill in missing letters. For example, 'fai_' could be completed as 'fail' or 'fair'; 'wro_' could be 'wrong' or 'wrote.' Those using red pens completed 28 percent more word-stems with words related to errors and poor performance than did people using black pens. 'The idea is if you are holding a red pen, the failure-related words come to mind more easily,' says Slepian."[16]

Isn't that interesting?

And other studies have produced similar results.

That got me thinking.

Am I a "red pen" person?

Do I look for opportunities to call out the weaknesses of the people around me?

Do I relish correcting their every error?

Am I the self-proclaimed expert in too many conversations?

Do I enjoy the bright red strokes a little too much?

Often, I do. Not always, but too often.

I tend to see shortcomings before I see strengths. Quicker to criticize than to compliment.

The problem is "red pen" people never seem to run out of ink.

I don't want to be that way.

I'm putting my red pen down.

Bending Steel

One winter our family took a blacksmithing class together.

Tony, our instructor, handed us each a steel rod about eight inches long.

"In the next two hours," he said, "we are going to turn this shapeless piece of metal into a beautiful piece of art."

We put on our fireproof gloves and safety goggles and Tony led us to the furnace. Steel, it turns out, is not all that malleable.

It doesn't bend easily – even under tremendous weight. That's why they use it to build bridges and skyscrapers.

But, when immersed in a white-hot fire, the steel begins, almost imperceptibly, to soften.

We plunged our rods into the burning coals and waited.

Once they were glowing red, we took them to our anvils and began hammering and bending them into something else – something new.

I only had a few seconds to work before the steel cooled and it needed to, once again, return to the fire. It felt like a long time before there was any noticeable progress. But, little by little, it began to change shape.

As I pounded at the stubborn metal, I thought about the stubbornness of my heart. I thought about how unbending I can be. I thought about how, sometimes, the only way for God to mold and shape me is to immerse me in fire.

By the end, the steel was almost unrecognizable. The old useless gray rod had been worked into a piece of artistic twists and elegant curves.

God – graciously – doesn't always soften us by fire. He doesn't only mold and shape us in midst of the flames.

But, when He does, I don't want to resist. I want to take the fire when it comes.

I want to be softened.

God, soften me.

Circles

Let's try an experiment.

You'll need a bandana, sidewalk chalk, an empty parking lot, and a friend (to make sure you don't walk into a wall).

Draw a long straight line and stand at one end. Your task is simple. Walk that straight line blindfolded.

You can't do it – at least not for more than a couple of yards.

Researchers have tested this and found that absent external reference points people will walk – get this – in *circles*, all the while convinced they are walking in a straight line.

What researchers don't know is *why* this happens.

I don't know either.

But it got me thinking.

Could it be that we weren't made to be *internally* directed? Could it be that we were made to orient ourselves to an *external* reference?

Here's what I've noticed.

When I take my eyes off of God – off of who He is, what He has done, and who He created me to be – I end up walking in circles.

I don't need just any external reference. I need *Him*.

He is the standard by which every part of me is measured. There is no other. That's why the author of Hebrews encouraged us to keep our eyes on Jesus, "the champion who initiates and perfects our faith."[17]

He is the beginning and the end and everything in between.

He has His heart set on me – and on *you*.

Let's stop walking in circles.

Let's set our eyes – and our hearts – on *Him*.

Spiritual Stockholm Syndrome

Four employees were held hostage at a Stockholm bank in 1973 when a botched bank robbery turned into a six-day standoff between the captors and the police.

The incident, now decades past, would have been long forgotten save for an interesting twist.

The captors and captives *bonded*.

In fact, when one of the hostages spoke with the Swedish Prime Minister on the phone during the standoff, she said she trusted her captives fully, but feared she would die at the hands of the police.

She trusted her *captors* over her *liberators*.

The situation was so remarkable that it was dubbed "Stockholm Syndrome."

It describes the implausible love of a captive for his captor.

It's absurd.

But I get it.

Sin is *slavery*. It takes me captive. It holds me hostage.

Yet, I choose it. I submit to it. I even *love* it.

The Bible says that we all do.

It's *spiritual* Stockholm Syndrome.

We have a Liberator. He offers us freedom. He is decidedly on our side.

Let's call sin what it is – a Captor. Sin is not our ally. Sin is not our friend. It is our *captor*.

Let's abandon our spiritual Stockholm Syndrome – where we trust our oppressor.

Let's, instead, trust our Liberator. Let's love *Him*. Let's choose *Him*.

To do otherwise is absurd.

Stars and Legends

Blaze debuted at the Sundance Film Festival in 2018.

Director Ethan Hawke masterfully tells the story of Blaze Foley, a country singer/songwriter who had a lot of hard breaks, made a lot of poor decisions, and died too young – but wrote beautiful lyrics.

In one scene, Blaze and his wife are riding in the back of a pickup truck, dreaming about the future.

"You're going to be a star," she tells him.

"I don't want to be a star," he says.

"Stars are selfish. Stars shine for themselves. I want to be a legend. Legends are after something bigger than themselves. Legends write and play for others. Legends leave something that lasts."[18]

Stars and legends both shine.

The difference is for what purpose they shine.

To *be* seen or so that others *can* see.

To *be* served or *to* serve.

To be *self*-centered or to be *others*-centered.

Neither stars nor legends become such overnight.

Each comprises thousands of choices in thousands of mostly mundane moments.

One such moment is before you – and before me.

Let's make it legendary.

Grayscale

What is Christian maturity?

That's the question a seminary professor I once had posed to our class.

We sat in awkward silence for a moment before one brave soul raised his hand.

"Maturity is knowing how to navigate the gray," he said.

That may have been the most profound thing I learned all semester.

What he meant was there are a lot of gray issues in life – issues over which honest, intelligent Christians disagree.

Maturity is learning how to navigate those issues as Jesus would have us navigate them – with wisdom and love and respect.

However, I would make more explicit what I believe my classmate intended to imply in his definition.

Maturity is knowing how to navigate the gray *and* how to discern the black and white from the gray. Maturity is standing firm on the black and white *and* embracing freedom in the gray.

We tend, though, to either see the world as *entirely* black and white or as *entirely* gray.

The former is dogmatism. The latter is relativism.

Dogmatism leaves no room for honest debate or agreeable disagreement. It assumes than anyone with a dissenting view is ignorant or, perhaps, even malicious. Dogmatism, more often than not, is based on personal opinion, rather than objective truth. For example, there are Christians dogmatic about how they believe God created the universe. The black and white of Scripture is *that* God created the universe. The *how* is gray. But dogmatism is uncomfortable with gray and so tries to convert gray issues into black and white ones.

Relativism, on the other hand, leaves no room for conviction. If everything is gray, then right and wrong is wholly determined by the individual. That simply doesn't align with reality. It breaks down with the slightest push. For example, if I stole your wallet you would protest that what I did was wrong. But, if you're a good relativist, you'd have to admit that, though you'd *prefer* I not steal your wallet, I didn't do anything wrong. Maybe I believe stealing to be right. It's all relative. It's all gray.

There *is* truth. There *is* right and wrong. There *is* black and white.

But not *everything* is black and white. God has given us enormous freedom within the confines of His objective reality.

Christian maturity is learning which is which and living accordingly. Christian maturity is learning how to navigate *every* issue in such a way that we represent and reflect the heart and character of *Christ*.

As Augustine once wrote, "In essentials, unity; in non-essentials, liberty; in all things, charity."

Faithful Servants

February 21, 2018 was an important day.

Billy Graham celebrated his first day in Heaven. Graham was (and is now more than ever) totally devoted to Jesus.

He gave his life to spreading the message that in Jesus – and only in Jesus – we can be forgiven of our sins and enjoy a reconciled relationship with the God of the universe.

The impact Graham had on our world is nearly impossible to overstate. Through his preaching and teaching, God changed the hearts and lives of countless men and women.

He wasn't a perfect man, by any means. But he was a man committed to his Savior. When I heard that he had passed away, I could almost hear Jesus saying, "Well done, good and faithful servant."

Our loss is his gain.

But February 21, 2018 was important for another reason.

It was a celebration of a different sort.

It was my Mama's birthday.

Most of the world has never heard her name. She has never preached before millions or written a best-seller or met with international leaders.

But as I thought about the impact that Billy Graham has had on the world, I thought also about the impact *she* has had on *my* world.

I've watched her begin every day by spending time with Jesus – listening to Him and talking with Him as with her best friend.

I've watched her open her home to hundreds of people.

I've watched her prepare thousands of meals (and thousands of batches of cookies) for family and friends and neighbors and just about anyone else that God allowed to cross her path.

I've watched her go through cancer with gratitude for each day and then seek out other women going through that same hell, so she could encourage them and pray for them.

I've watched her give generously of herself and whatever else she had to those in need.

I've watched her humbly serve without complaining even when those of us she serves fail to serve her in return – or, too often, to even thank her.

To have a heart like that.

She teaches me more about the love of Jesus every single day.

She makes me want to know Him more and love Him better every single day.

I'm less like Jesus than I want to be, but more like Him than I would have been without her.

Here's the point.

There is more than one way to be a good and faithful servant of Jesus.

Billy Graham was faithful to the call God made on his life and, as a result, God used him powerfully.

My Mama – Chrissy – has been faithful to the call God made on her life and, as a result, God has used her and *is* using her powerfully.

We need the Billys.

We also need the Chrissys.

I, for one, am grateful for both.

You are so missed, Billy.

I'm grateful for you, Mama.

Here's the problem with S.E.P.s.

If we are *all* editing them out, then "somebody else's problem" becomes "nobody's problem."

It doesn't take jumping around and waving our arms and blinking a lot to see our S.E.P.s.

It just takes paying attention to what's right in front of us.

Let's pay attention.

The Aim of Faithfulness

When I stepped up to take my first shot, I noticed that the target was kind of, well, blurry.

I hadn't picked up a bow and arrow in years, but I didn't remember the concentric circles having fuzzy edges.

As it turns out, I had forgotten to put in my contacts. This happens more often than it should. How I didn't notice they were missing before that moment is beyond me (I had, after all, *driven* to the shooting range).

I didn't hit the target once.

I hit the floor a few times, almost took out a ceiling light, and I'm pretty sure I got a piece of the target three down from mine.

But where I was *supposed* to be aiming?

No such luck.

After a series of failed attempts to land an arrow *anywhere* near the target, I went out to my car to see if I had a backup pair of glasses.

I did.

They changed everything.

I could see the crisp lines of the target clearly. I knew right where I was aiming.

Even with my glasses on, it still took a while to get the hang of it.

But, as time when on, as I kept trying, assessing my shot, and correcting my aim, I got better.

By the end, I was certainly no Robin Hood, but I had managed to hit the mark with far more consistency and precision than when I began.

I wonder if that's how we sometimes approach faithfulness to God.

The target is blurry. We're not entirely sure where we're aiming, so we end up hurling arrows in the general direction we think they're supposed to be heading.

But, day after day, month after month, year after year, we're not getting any closer to the mark.

What if we are in dire need of contacts – or backup glasses?

What if we allowed *God* to correct our blurry vision?

The crisp lines of the target would start to come into focus. We'd find that the aim of faithfulness to God is made clear.

Jesus was once asked, "Which commandment is the most important of all?"

In other words, "Jesus, what is the aim of a faithful life? What is the target of obedience?"

"The most important commandment is this: 'Listen, O Israel! The Lord our God is the one and only Lord. And you must love the Lord your God with all your heart, all your soul, all your mind, and all your strength.' The second is equally important: 'Love your neighbor as yourself.' No other commandment is greater than these."[20]

Love God. Love people.

That is the aim of faithfulness to God.

The question is whether or not we will land closer to the target today than we did yesterday.

Hurried

The gate attendant announced that we would be boarding shortly, so I put my book away and got in line. When they called my group, three *grown men* shoved past me – literally knocking me over (and I'm not exaggerating here – I mean I *literally* fell down) and tipping my luggage to the ground – in order to get on the plane first.

We were in the *first* boarding group. We had *assigned* seats. The overhead bin space was *not* going to be full. There was *no* reason to hurry.

I'd be lying if I said I wasn't annoyed. I'd also be lying if I said I wasn't tempted to give them a piece of my mind peppered with a couple choice words (I didn't).

Hurry is what we do.

I've been noticing the symptoms of hurry a lot lately.

I was in Utah for vacation, driving on a windy, narrow mountain road with my siblings, when a truck came barreling up from behind. Our pace (the speed limit) was evidently too slow for him, so he swerved into the opposite lane to get around us. Mercifully, no one was coming, because he certainly wouldn't have been able to see around the bend if anyone was. As it turns out, he was going the same place we were. He "beat" us there by seconds.

I was trying on a shirt at a small boutique later that week. Through the dressing room curtain, I heard a customer tell the saleswoman that she was ready to try on her clothes. The saleswoman told her that there was only one dressing room (mine, for the moment) and, as soon as I finished, she would be able to use it. She kindly offered to hold the woman's clothing if she wanted to continue browsing while she waited.

"But I'm ready to try my clothes on *now*," said the clearly impatient shopper. "So, what do you suggest I do?"

I confess that a part of me wanted to take my sweet time in that dressing room. (You're really getting a glimpse into my sinful heart here.)

Hurry is just what we do. It's a habit. Often, we don't even realize we're doing it, much less know *why* we're doing it.

"Hurry," writes John Ortberg, "is not just a disordered schedule. Hurry is a disordered heart."[21]

I don't know what's disordered in your heart. I know – at least in my more honest moments – what's disordered in mine.

I prioritize productivity over people and movement over memories. I think more about what's ahead of me than what's right in front of me.

Life is short. Too often, it's way too short.

Let's slow down. Let's learn to wait. Let's find out what we have been missing. Let's take a deep breath. Let's stop and, quite literally, smell the roses. Let's get our hearts back on track.

Choosing Joy

I met Margie on a flight from Charlotte to St. Louis. She and Jackie, her best friend of sixty years, were on their way back from visiting Margie's daughter.

I took the aisle seat and prepared to avoid two hours of small talk by pulling out my headphones.

Margie, without introducing herself, turned to me and said, "Now, are you going to cause any trouble on this flight? Because this row only has enough room for one troublemaker, and I've already got that role covered."

"No," I smiled. "The flight attendant asked me sit here, so I could keep you in line."

I put my headphones away. We talked for the rest of the flight.

Margie told me she wanted to get a BB gun so she could scare off the squirrels that congregated outside her apartment window, but Jackie wouldn't let her.

"It's just not safe, Marge," Jackie piped in. "You're a terrible shot and you're liable to hit someone."

Marge rolled her eyes and looked to me for support. I gladly complied. "You should definitely get a BB gun, Marge. Jackie, mind your own business."

Margie told me about the time she and Ruthie mooned Jackie and Franny when they were out golfing. Jackie, without looking up from her book, said, "Seventy-nine is too old to be mooning people, Marge. Nobody wants to see your wrinkly behind."

Margie leaned over and told me not to listen to Jackie. "She reads those dirty romance novels. You can't trust her." This time, Jackie looked up. "I'm reading John Grisham! Marge, don't tell people I'm reading dirty books!"

I laughed at the banter between these old friends. Jackie went back to her book and Marge and I went back to talking.

Marge hasn't had an easy life. When her first husband lost his battle to cancer, she took a job in the hotel management industry that kept her on the road and away from home most of the time. She remarried in her mid-fifties and enjoyed two decades with her second husband before he lost his battle to Parkinson's.

Margie is eighty-seven now. She moved into assisted living a couple months ago. Her health is declining and the pain in her left hip has stripped her of the independence she loved.

But she has no complaints and no regrets.

I asked her how she had cultivated such a joyful spirit despite all the heartache she had experienced.

S.E.P.s

I love the writing of Douglas Adams. If you haven't read *The Hitchhiker's Guide to the Galaxy* series, I would highly recommend it. It's fantastic.

The story begins with a man named Ford Prefect rescuing his friend, Arthur Dent, from a doomed Earth. As it turns out, the Vogons, a rather unpleasant race of aliens, intended to demolish it to make way for an intergalactic bypass.

Ford and Arthur manage to catch a ride on a spaceship called the Heart of Gold. The series documents their many adventures as they explore the galaxy.

On one such adventure, Ford and Arthur mistakenly go too far back in time and find themselves, once again, on Earth (before it was destroyed) at a cricket match.

Arthur is beside himself with joy at being back on his home planet and Ford, who isn't actually from Earth, is behaving quite oddly.

"He was waving his hands in sharp movements across his face, ducking down behind some people, leaping up behind others, then standing still and blinking a lot…

'Something's on your mind, isn't it?' said Arthur.

'I think,' said Ford… 'that there's an S.E.P. over there.'

He pointed. Curiously enough, the direction he pointed in was not the one in which he was looking."

Arthur inquires as to what, exactly, an S.E.P is.

"'Somebody Else's Problem,' said Ford... 'An S.E.P... is something that we can't see, or don't see, or our brain doesn't let us see, because we think that it's somebody else's problem... The brain just edits it out; it's like a blind spot. If you look at it directly you won't see it unless you know precisely what it is. Your only hope is to catch it by surprise out of the corner of your eye.'"[19]

The S.E.P. turns out to be a spaceship belonging to a man named Slartibartfast, but, if you want to know who he is and why he landed his spaceship at a cricket match, you'll just have to get the book and read it for yourself (I promise it's worth it).

It is the concept of an S.E.P. that I find so fascinating.

Ford, at least, understood that his brain was editing out the S.E.P.s and, so, knew to look for them. Arthur, on the other hand, had no clue that there might be more to the world than what his brain was processing.

I'm, too often, more like Arthur than I am Ford.

I'm unaware that I'm unaware. I miss so much that is right before me because I'm not looking for it.

I miss opportunities to listen, to serve, to give, to love.

Those opportunities are just "somebody else's problem."

"God has been so good to me," she said. "Even in the darkest times, He gave me reason to be grateful. You can't choose *what* God will ask you walk through, but you can choose *how* you walk through it. Oh, there's been heartache, to be sure. I've cried a lot of tears and I still deeply miss the people I've lost. It's just that I decided a long time ago I didn't want to waste a single minute of my time dwelling on what might or should have been. Cranky old people start out as cranky young people. Don't be a cranky young person, Casey."

I won't be.

Thank you, Margie.

I'm glad I put the headphones away.

Self-Forgetfulness

I had the honor of meeting Aidan Mackey in England during a period I spent in Oxford studying the writings of C.S. Lewis.

I had never heard of him before, but I learned quickly that he is regarded as the foremost scholar on G.K. Chesterton.

Aidan did not claim such an honor for himself. He was adamant that he was neither a scholar nor an academic in the proper sense. But he was, after all, president of the G.K. Chesterton Study Centre and if the British Library entrusts you with eight boxes of the renowned Chesterton's personal belongings, you're a scholar – proper or not.

Aidan served in the British Air Force during World War II. He said he was stationed in Africa because it was where they believed he would do the least damage.

After the war he spent most of his career as a teacher and headmaster. He had seven daughters and speaks of them with warmth and pride and delightful British humor.

Aidan told me that when a young man asked for his daughter's hand in marriage, he said, "I would love to give my daughter to you in marriage, but I need to know that you can provide for a family. After all, there are nine of us."

When I asked how he came to be the foremost scholar on G.K. Chesterton, he, again, denied it and gave the humblest answer I could have imagined.

"There have been many unfair things that have happened in my life," he said. "Mostly to my benefit."

Aidan takes no credit whatever.

He isn't suffering from low self-esteem. He's embracing self-forgetfulness.

When I think about the unfair things in my life, I focus on things that have *not* been to my benefit.

And I'm happy to take personal credit for those things that *were* to my benefit.

But that credit is not mine to take.

Every good thing I have has been given to me by God.

I can decide what I do with what I've been given, but I can't take credit for the opportunities I've been given.

I could use a little more self-forgetfulness.

I could do to express gratitude for the graciously unfair opportunities that God has brought into my life.

I could do to learn and live the humility of Aidan.

Heroes

I was introduced to the writing of C.S. Lewis when I was a junior in college. His work has since profoundly influenced my faith in Christ, perhaps more so than anyone else.

Mere Christianity captured my mind and invited me to think reasonably about what I believe. *The Chronicles of Narnia* captured my heart and drew me into a deeper love for Jesus. *The Weight of Glory* compelled me to consider the responsibility I have to others. *The Screwtape Letters* unveiled the subtly of spiritual warfare. *A Grief Observed* taught me to pray raw and honest prayers to a God who can handle my brokenness and even my anger and disappointment at a broken world.

Lewis is, undoubtedly, one of my heroes in the faith.

I never got to meet Lewis. He passed away decades before I was born.

But I got to meet another hero of mine during the time I spent in England.

You've probably never heard of him.

His name is Walter Hooper.

Hooper was Lewis's secretary the last year of his life.

The publishing company that put out Lewis' books was planning to pull them from print, as was, at the time, common practice when an author passed away.

Hooper, a native of North Carolina, resolved to stay in England and dedicated himself to keeping the legacy of Lewis alive. He fought to keep Lewis' writing in print, and he succeeded. He also compiled and published thousands of letters written by Lewis.

It's not a stretch to suggest that if we didn't have Hooper, we wouldn't have Lewis. That is, he would not be as widely known, read, or regarded as he is today.

It's tempting to envy how God has gifted another. It's tempting to become discontent in how God has gifted us. It's tempting to succumb to the notion that those who receive recognition and acclamation for their influence, like Lewis, are the ones who are *really* making a difference in the world.

For the Christian community to function as it was intended, we need everyone pursuing a unified purpose by way of their distinct giftedness. We are not to compete with one another but to complement one another.

Lewis used his gifts, and Hooper used his. God is still using Lewis to change hearts and minds. God used Hooper to make such change possible.

That's why Walter Hooper is also, though for different reasons, my hero and why it was such an honor to meet him. I owe him a debt of gratitude for humbly using his gifts so that another could use theirs.

Enjoy the Ride

Our whole crew was supposed to arrive in Nairobi on the same flight.

But we got separated at the passport checkpoint in the Paris airport.

I waited a couple of minutes, but as we were already in danger of missing our flight, I ran, *Home Alone* style, to the gate and trusted they'd meet me there.

I got to the gate just in time for the final boarding call. There was no sign of my companions. I boarded at the instance of the ticketing agent who warned me that the doors were about to close.

Maybe they were already on the plane. Maybe they beat me there. Maybe a kind airport employee had picked them up on one of those little airport golfcarts and taken a shortcut to get them to the gate on time.

I searched the plane.

They were nowhere to be found.

I heard the door slam, and the flight attendants instructed all passengers to take their seats.

I was off to Kenya.

Alone.

When I arrived in Nairobi, I found out that none of my bags had been checked to my plane. I did manage to contact my companions, who had gotten on another flight scheduled to arrive the next morning. When everyone finally got in, only four of our twelve bags – most of which were filled with donations for the ministry we were visiting – had made it. We still didn't have the other eight, nor were we entirely certain where they were.

It's not an adventure if everything goes as planned.

I've had a lot of adventures.

Every adventure – every delayed flight, every lost bag, every obstacle – reminds me that I have far less control over my own life than I believe I do.

What I *do* have control over is how I respond to those obstacles.

I can complain about the unsympathetic ticketing agent that wouldn't hold the plane, or I can thank God that we all made is safely to Nairobi.

I can grumble about the incompetent employees that lost our luggage, or I can thank God for providing just enough and recognize that I can get by on a lot less than I think I can.

I can let my frustration get the better of me, or I can enjoy the ride.

Every unpredictable minute of it.

Everything

I had been in Kenya just shy of a week.

I was spending time at a wonderful place called the Hope Center.

The children there have had difficult lives. Most of them have been orphaned. Many were living on the streets. The Hope Center takes them in and provides them with their basic necessities – clothing, shelter, food, and an education.

But they still have so little, at least by American standards.

Each child has a single trunk that holds all of their worldly possessions. They sleep two to a bed under mosquito nets to avoid contracting malaria. They have latrines instead of toilets. They wash their clothes in basins and hang them out to dry since they don't have washing machines or dryers. They wash their bodies by pouring buckets of water over themselves since they don't have showers.

We spent time getting to know the children better – asking them to tell us about themselves.

I asked one little girl if she could have one wish what it would be.

She thought for a moment.

"Well," she said, "I already have everything."

She thought a little more.

"But I would wish to help people that *don't* have everything. I want to help the poor, the needy, and the orphans."

Cue overwhelming conviction.

She is poor. *She* is needy. *She* is an orphan.

She's right, though.

She does have everything – everything she needs.

The Hope Center takes wonderful care of these children. They are clothed, fed, and educated. They are treated with dignity. They are encouraged. They are loved. They are a family.

At the Hope Center, they are teaching the children that everything they have – every opportunity – is a gift from God. They are teaching them that they were created with a plan and for a purpose. They are teaching them that, though they may be orphans, they are the children of a good and gracious Father.

That's why this sweet girl doesn't see all she lacks.

She sees all she has been given.

And because she sees all she has been given, she sees all she has to give.

I usually have it backwards. I don't see all that I have been given. I only see what I lack. I confuse *needs* with *wants*. I don't believe I already have everything.

Even though I do. Even though I have more than all of these children *combined*.

They teach me the meaning of contentment. They are grateful for what they have. They are generous with what they have. They are kind. They are joyful.

I want to say with this beautiful little girl, "I already have *everything*."

Because I have Jesus.

And He is more than enough.

Clarabelle, Zazu, and Ludwig von Drake

Annie (my oldest niece) loves everything Disney (except for the "scary" parts – like the wolves in Snow White and the sharks in Finding Nemo).

Her favorite characters, though, are the most obscure ones.

Oh, she likes Mickey and Minnie and all of the princesses. But she *loves* the characters everyone else seems to overlook.

Her first love was Clarabelle the cow.

Do you know who that is? Neither did I until Annie started watching the Mickey Mouse Clubhouse.

Clarabelle shows up about once every ten episodes and makes "udderly ridiculous" cow puns.

When her Daddy (my brother) got her a stuffed Clarabelle, Annie put her hands over her mouth in delighted awe. She even got a little shy and backed away – so overwhelmed was she by the thought of having her very own Clarabelle to snuggle.

Then she saw the Lion King. She thought Simba and Nala were fine. She thought Timon and Pumba were alright. But she *loved* Zazu – the annoying, uptight hornbill.

Who loves Zazu?! No one. Except this girl. She loved Zazu so much that she went as Zazu for Halloween. Since no child has ever wanted to go as Zazu, my Mama and Annie's Mama had to make her costume from scratch.

Now she's into Ludwig von Drake (better known as Scrooge McDuck). He, like Clarabelle and Zazu, is a rather obscure character. She has been doing extra chores to earn enough money to buy a von Drake toy when we go to Disney World. Prayers that they even *have* a von Drake toy.

Here's the point.

I *love* how Annie loves the obscure – the fringe – characters. I love how she isn't enamored with the big shots. I love how she doesn't care if it's "cool" to like them.

I hope she always loves those on the fringe – always loves those living in the margins. I hope she always cares for those that everyone else seems to overlook. I hope she's never too "cool" to befriend the "uncool."

Because that's how our God has loved us. He loves the "main characters," to be sure. But He's equally enamored by the least, the overlooked, the forgotten.

And He calls us to love the least, the overlooked, the forgotten, too.

Don't Regret Your London

I was one of those college students that couldn't commit to a major. I was interested in so many subjects. I started off studying audio production, but it was too technical. I switched to photography but realized it would be hard to make a living as a photographer. So, I switched to exercise and nutrition, but it was a lot of science and I don't have a scientific mind. I went through three degrees in two years.

Then, junior year, I had an opportunity to study in Colorado Springs at the Focus on the Family Leadership Institute. Though Focus is still doing incredible things, the Leadership Institute shut down a couple years ago. I still dream of being a part of its resurrection.

But that's not the point.

The point is while I was studying in Colorado, I felt God calling me into ministry. I didn't know what that meant. All I knew was that God was calling me to give my life to serving His people.

I went back home and decided to pursue a degree in psychology. I thought maybe God was calling me to be a counselor. I took one counseling course and realized I was *not* wired to be a counselor but with three semesters left was already barely going to graduate on time. So, I finished my psychology degree and resolved to figure it out upon graduation.

I honestly didn't know what to do. I was serving in the youth ministry at the church I was attending and really fell in love with this crew of middle school girls.

Do you remember middle school? It is *rough*. It's that awkward period between being a child and a teenager and, man, it's just a confusing time. I loved those girls because I remembered what it was like to be them. I thought maybe God was calling me into student ministry. (He wasn't, but that's another story for another time.)

Then, the summer before my senior year, I went to a leadership conference all on my own. I knew no one. I was staying in a hotel by myself. I was just there to listen and learn.

But there was this group attending the conference – and they noticed I was sitting alone. They invited me to sit with them, hung out with me during the breaks, and took me to dinner (and even paid for me) every night. They were so kind and quickly felt like friends.

They asked me about where I felt God was calling me. I told them what I'd been thinking. It turns out they were from London (I'd already gathered that from their accents) and, lo and behold, they were looking for a student ministry leader. They offered me the job on the spot. They'd pay to move me to London, and I could start whenever I wanted.

I said no.

I had another year left to finish my degree and didn't feel qualified to accept the position they were offering. And, to be honest, I was afraid to move so far away. I was twenty-one and still felt so young.

I'm really grateful for where I am and what I'm doing. I wouldn't trade it for anything. I'm near family. I get to hang out with my nieces and nephews every week. I love my friends. I love my church. I love what I do and I love how I spend my days.

But I've thought about that offer at least once a month for the last fifteen years.

I wonder what it would have been like to just take it – to say yes to that adventure. I don't regret the life I've had. But I *wonder*. And I kind of wish I'd taken the leap.

Most choices aren't irreversible. If it's not the right fit, you can change course. But there are opportunities that come once in a lifetime. If you take them and it's not right, you can opt out. But if you don't take them, you can't get them back.

I don't know what opportunities you have. You may not feel qualified. You may be scared. You may feel like once you take it there's no turning back. That's usually not the case.

I love the life I have. I am so grateful for the entire journey.

But I wish I'd gone to London. I wish I'd gone on that adventure.

Don't regret – don't wonder about – your London.

All In

Willie is a cab driver in Chicago. He's in his mid-fifties now and has been transporting people all over the city for upwards of twenty years.

I met Willie when he drove me from downtown to the O'Hare International Airport.

We made small talk for a bit. He asked where I was from and what I was doing in Chicago. I asked how long he'd live in the city and how he liked it.

He told me that prior to becoming a cab driver he'd been a professional boxer.

He told me all about his training, his travels, and his career. He talked about the discipline required to stay in peak condition and the drive to be constantly learning and improving.

Then he said something that has stayed with me.

"Boxing takes total commitment. You can't be lax. If you slack off in training, you'll get knocked out in the ring. No man can live two lives. Either you're all in or you're out."

I'm no boxer (shocking, I know), but I still think about that all the time.

I think about what it means to be all in.

I think about whether I'm trying to live two lives – trying to spread my attention and energy in too many directions, trying to do and be more than God has called me to do and be.

I can't say I'm at risk of getting knocked out on a daily basis – the way Willie was during his boxing career.

But I am at risk of making less of a difference in the world. I am at risk of being less of the person God has created me to be. I am at risk of doing less for the Kingdom of God than God intends.

I want to finish this life with cramping muscles and with lungs gasping for air because I ran so hard after what God called me to.

I don't want to live two lives. I want to be all in.

Scaling Up

The year after I graduated from college a friend and I backpacked through Europe (yes, we were stereotypical millennials in our early twenties).

We started in London, made our way down to Paris, enjoyed an extended stay in Switzerland where another friend was then living, and wrapped up in Rome. We packed in a lot of experiences, made a lot of memories, and learned a lot of lessons.

I particularly remember visiting the Louvre in Paris. We only had a couple days in the city and so couldn't spend too much time meandering through the massive art museum. We really only wanted to see one exhibit.

The Mona Lisa.

It took us thirty minutes or so to make our way from the front of the museum to the giant room dedicated to Da Vinci's masterpiece.

We stopped along the way to admire other paintings and sculptures, but the closer we got to the Mona Lisa, the more excited we got and the more quickly we moved through the other exhibits.

Then, there it was. The Mona Lisa.

We stood there in awe.

But then the awe wore off.

It was enclosed in a huge glass case with armed guards stationed on all sides.

I was struck by how small it was.

I mean, *really* small.

I don't know the exact dimensions, but I'm pretty sure I have a coloring page from my niece larger than the Mona Lisa (and personally way more valuable).

Now, don't get me wrong. The Mona Lisa is a masterpiece and now, looking back ten years later, I wish I'd enjoyed the moment a little more. But here's what I thought as we made our way back out to the Paris streets.

So often I think something is a lot bigger than it is. I think something is a lot harder than it is. I think something is more of a problem than it is. I scale it up in my mind.

But then I get up close and it turns out to be much smaller than I imagined. All of the anticipation – all of the worry, all of the anxiety – was a waste.

I bet I'm not the only one. I bet you've experienced that before. I bet you've looked back on a situation and realized it wasn't quite as big as you imagined it would be.

We all *have* faced and *will* face our share of truly big problems.

Let's not scale up the small ones.

Blessed are the Flexible

I've spent a good bit of time in the Middle East – traveling around Egypt, Jordan, Israel, and a little time in Turkey and Greece.

I've traveled with, in my humble opinion, many of the best teachers, best guides, and best drivers in the world.

They know what they're doing. They have flights and hotels booked. They have sites scheduled out. They have a full itinerary planned.

But inevitably things go wrong.

Flash floods wash out a highway. A herd of sheep blocks the road and delays our departure or arrival. A site is closed when it was scheduled to be open.

You might think I'm joking, but I'm not. I've experienced every one of these scenarios and more.

As a Jordanian guide of mine once said, "If it doesn't make sense, you're in the Middle East."

But the organization I've so often traveled with has a saying that puts it all in perspective.

"Blessed are the flexible, for they shall be bent but not broken."

That's more than a principle for travel.

That's a principle for *life*.

Flash floods *will* wash out the highways. Herds of sheep *will* keep you from coming and going. Sites *will* be closed when you're hoping to visit.

Metaphorically, of course.

(But also, literally if you plan to visit the Middle East.)

Here's the point.

Blessed are the flexible, for they shall be bent but not broken.

What if we lived our lives with that perspective?

What if we resolved to be flexible – confident that we could be bent but, by the grace of God, not broken?

If These Walls Could Talk

You've heard that phrase before, right?

It's usually uttered at an old or historic building.

"If these walls could talk, imagine the stories they would tell."

Well, in Egypt, the walls really *do* talk.

Not out loud, of course.

But if you visit any of the temple ruins – which are absolutely colossal – you'll noticed that just about every inch of every wall bears ornate carvings and intricate designs.

These carvings, though, are not merely aesthetic.

They are intended to tell the story of the Pharaoh's victories.

They declare his power.

They sing his praises and proclaim his glory.

As I stood at one such temple – Medinet Habu, built by and dedicated to Ramesses III – I thought about the "walls," if you will, of my life.

I thought about what stories *I'm* telling.

Am I telling the story of *my* victories – or God's?

Am I declaring *my* power – or God's?

Am I hoping that people will sing *my* praises and proclaim *my* glory – or God's?

The Bible says that we are stones in the temple of the Holy Spirit.

I want every inch of *my* stone to be carved with the story of who *He* is and what *He* has done.

Hey Patrick. It's Grandpa.

I don't answer phone calls from numbers I don't recognize. I figure if it's important they'll leave a message, and I can return it as soon as I'm able.

The last couple of weeks I've gotten a series of calls from Branson, Missouri. I don't know anyone in Branson, so I didn't answer. I assumed it was a telemarketer.

But the other night, the caller left a message.

"Hey Patrick. It's Grandpa. I just wanted to see how you were doing. I miss you. Call me when you can. I love you. Bye."

I called back.

The same sweet voice that left the message on my phone answered my call.

I explained who I was and told him that, unfortunately, this was not Patrick's number.

"Oh, thank you so much for calling, sweetie," he said. "I was so worried that he was just too busy to talk to me anymore."

That broke my heart.

And it convicted me.

I've lost most of my grandparents. But I still have parents. Siblings. Nieces and nephews. Aunts and uncles. Cousins. Friends.

I'm ashamed to admit I've often been "too busy" for the relationships that I say matter most to me.

I don't want the people I love to ever feel like I'm too busy to talk to them.

No, I won't always be able to shoot the breeze. No, I can't always interrupt my day just to chat.

I have to have boundaries in order to do what God has called me to do. I'm not suggesting you welcome every interruption to your day. I know I can't.

But I want to be available for relationship. I want to know how the people I love are doing. I want to be there when they need me.

Patrick didn't know his Grandpa was trying to call.

But don't be too busy to take that call when you get it.

And - I'm speaking more to myself than anyone here - don't be too busy to pick up the phone and call the people you love.

Conclusion

The world is crowded with the presence of God. He is there – incognito.

But He's not hiding from us.

He's *inviting* us to pay attention, to open our eyes, to come awake.

I hope this little book encouraged you to pay attention. I hope you begin to see Him in every moment of every day.

And, when you do, I hope you tell *your* stories so that others might begin to see Him, too.

Bibliography

1. C.S. Lewis. *Letters to Malcolm* (Geoffrey Bles, 1964).
2. David Grann. *The Lost City of Z* (Doubleday, 2009).
3. "Money." *The Office*, created by Greg Daniels, Season 4, Episode 7, NBC, 2007.
4. Tim Kreider. *We Learn Nothing* (Simon & Schuster Paperbacks, 2012).
5. 1 Corinthians 1:18. *New Living Translation* (Tyndale House Publishers, 2015).
6. Brian Regan. *Live from Radio Music Hall* (November 2015).
7. Mary Taylor. *Borden of Yale '09* (China Inland Mission, 1951).
8. Noah Webster. *Webster's Dictionary* (G&C Merriam Co, 1913).
9. G.K. Chesterton. *Orthodoxy* (originally published in 1908; republished independently in 2017).
10. Jim David. *Garfield* (October 1989). You can see the complete comic strip by going to http://i.imgur.com/wQxo6.jpg.
11. Philippians 2:14-16. *New International Version* (Biblica, Inc. 2011).
12. Conn Iggulden. *The Emperor Series* (Delacorte Press, 2014).
13. Jim Gaffigan. *Beyond the Pale* (Netflix, 2005).
14. Mona Simpson. "A Sister's Eulogy for Steve Jobs." *The New York Times* (October 30, 2011).
15. Scott Adams. *Dilbert* (April 24, 2015).
16. Marjarie Howard. "Red Ink is Bad News." *Tufts Journal* (June 16, 2010).
17. Hebrews 12:2. *New Living Translation* (Tyndale House Publishers, 2015).
18. *Blaze*. Directed by Ethan Hawke. IFC Films. 2018.
19. Douglas Adams. *Life, the Universe and Everything* (Del Rey, 1997).
20. Mark 12:29-31. *New Living Translation* (Tyndale House Publishers, 2015).
21. John Ortberg. *The Life You've Always Wanted* (Zondervan, 2002).

Made in the USA
Monee, IL
12 May 2021